POEMS AND STORIES

About  and ,
and Various "Critters."

PAT MORRELL-DONNELLY

AuthorHouse™
1663 Liberty Drive
Bloomington, IN 47403
www.authorhouse.com
Phone: 1 (800) 839-8640

Published by AuthorHouse 02/21/2019

ISBN: 978-1-5462-7446-9 (sc)
ISBN: 978-1-5462-7445-2 (e)

Library of Congress Control Number: 2019900075

Print information available on the last page.

This book is printed on acid-free paper.

authorHOUSE®

Contents

Acknowledgements:

Most of the pictures, herein, were taken by Pat's husband, Alan (Don) Donnelly.

The pictures of MoJo and MaJor were provided by Peggy and Billy Wiggens.

The pictures of Star, Scoobie, Cassie, Pearl, and Meagan,
were provided by Sondra and Jerry Fairman.

The picture of Jack, the cat, provided by Janet Philpott.

Dedication:

This book is dedicated to Pat's husband, Alan B. (Don) Donnelly,

who is always supportive in whatever crazy dream/book, Pat comes up with.

To Pat's sister, Sondra Fairman, who helped with the numbering of all the pictures.

And, to all of those that have had animals they loved and lost.

About the Author:

Pat was born in Texas, and raised during the 1930's depression era. Her family had little in the way of material things. There was no indoor plumbing, running water, or electricity. The toilet, ("out-house,") was "out behind the back of the house."

Pat's family moved to California when she was fourteen. She immediately found a job working four hours a day, attending school four hours a day.

After graduating High School, at age sixteen, Pat was able to work full time. In those days people understood if they wanted something, anything monetarily, in life, you went out and worked for it. There was no welfare, no "give away" programs. No "free lunch."

After working at various jobs such as office work, modeling in San Francisco, Oakland, and Los Angeles, Pat worked over fifty one years as a Realtor, in the real estate profession, in Northern California.

Pat holds the unique distinction of being the only member of S.A.C.B.O.R, (Southern Alameda County Board Of Realtors,) to be honored "Miss Realtor," in a contest in 1960.

Pat has had articles and poems published in the "RealToro" Magazine, SACAR Realtor Guide, SACBOR TODAY, real estate publications. Her poems are used in Church Bulletins. Over forty poems have been read at Memorial and Funeral Services.

Pat published five books in seven years. "The Climb Up Life's Mountain," "Poems For Conservatives," "My Journey As A Realtor," "Honoring," "Poetry Breathes Life Into Bible Characters."

Pat writes "Personalized Poetry," and has written over 1600 poems. Patriotic, political, religious, motivational, inspirational.

Pat's has had "thank you" responses to her poems from the Queen of England, four U.S. Presidents, and two First Ladies.

Pat has written poems for a Governor, two Senators, three Congressmen, two Georgia Representatives. Plus, businesses, and restaurant chains.

Pat attended the Church of Christ, San Leandro, California, forty three years. Later, Vallejo, California. Presently C of C, Clermont, Georgia.

About the Book:

As the title states, this book contains stories and poems about cats and dogs. It relates the joy and pleasure they brought to their owners, and grief experienced when their pet passed away.

Pat has written these poems and stories, over time, about the animals life, and after some of the animals passed on.

The aim and purpose of the book is to help young people, starting with pre-teen, deal with grief through the reading of these stories and poems. It tells about the lives of these, special, cats and dogs.

This is a "self-help" book, of sorts. It is Pat's hope it will help pre-teen, teenagers, young adults, and even adults, that have lost pets, to know others have lost pets, how difficult it was, and how they dealt with loss of the pet.

Sometimes it helps, when one pet dies, to immediately get another one. That is sometimes difficult, as you feel no other pet can replace the one you lost.

It is a blessing that many people rescue pets from the "Pound," Animal Shelters, organizations such as, "Rescue Dogs," saving the pet from being euthanized.

Dogs and cats have meant much, to many, in different ways. They can be "therapy" to Senior Citizens, and "Shut-Ins." They lift us up when we are having a bad day.

The pets were given a good home, and they were given love and devotion. They were like family. They gave, in return, "unconditional love."

The book includes pictures of the cats and dogs that go along with the stories and poems.

For those of you that have had animals you loved, and lost, other animal lovers can feel your pain. Hopefully, these poems, and stories, will serve to let you know others grieve as you do. You are not alone.

Rainbow Bridge

Just this side of heaven is a place called Rainbow Bridge.

All the animals who had been ill and old are restored to health and vigor. Those who were hurt

or maimed are made whole and strong again. Just as we remember them in our dreams of days and

times gone by. The animals are happy and content, except for one small thing; they each miss someone very special to them, who had to be left behind.

Then you cross Rainbow Bridge together.

 Author unknown...

[1] This is a "portion" of a copyrighted poem, owned by an unknown Author.

Dopper - Relaxing

"Yes, that's me, Dopper, just relaxing. I found a good home. My Mom, Pat, thinks I'm special."

Dopper On Yellow Rug

"Where did my Mom ever find this yellow rug? It sure is bright, but it's softer than the floor."

Dopper and Midnight On Couch

"My brother, Midnight, and I, take naps together all the time. He is a nice big brother."

Dopper In Dresser Drawer

"It's cozy sleeping here in my Mom's dresser drawer. Her clothes are soft. No one bothers me here."

DOPPER-Kitty Cat

Funny name for a cat. Funny name for anyone. But, actually, Dopper came by her name quite honestly, or naturally. The name really fits her to a "T".

I had never been a "cat person." Once upon a time, many years ago, I had a dog. She was a small cocker spaniel, the "runt" of the litter. She was blonde and beautiful. Beautiful to me, of course. She was smart, and "human-like." Her name was Miss Priscilla, Prissy, for short. She was just six years old when she died, when I had to have her "put down."

When Prissy died I said I would never have another dog. It was too painful to lose her. She was like a child to me, and losing her was heartbreaking.

Things changed about five years ago, as far as having animals. A boy, down the block from our house, gave my husband a black kitten for Christmas. Not being a lover of cats I remarked, "What are we going to do with that kitten?" My husband's reply was, "We will make him a bed in the garage, and as soon as the weather is warmer we will put him outside." The garage was attached to the house, so it would be comfortable for him, out of the "elements."

Right away my husband said, "I am going to name the kitten, "Midnight." Midnight was all black with a touch of white under his chin. And, as some of you might have already guessed, before long, Midnight moved from the garage into the house. So much for putting him outside.

But, this story is not about Mr. Midnight, the "King of the Hill," the "Big Shot of the block," The "Big Shot" inside and outside of our home. He was our Mr. Independent, proud, beautiful, black cat.

This story is about "Dopper," the most loving, adorable, lovable, human-like, unusual cat—I'm sure that was ever born. Just my opinion, of course. Oh, she might not have been beautiful to others, not an outer-type beauty, a beauty that would call to her a lot of attention. Most people would not have given her a second look. But, her tiny face, and skinny frame was beautiful to me. She would look up at you, meow, and act just like she was trying to talk to you.

How she happened to come to our home, and choose us for her own, is quite a story. It will always and forevermore remain a mystery. My husband must have fed her, or left food on the back deck for Midnight. Otherwise, we have no idea what could have drawn her to our house. Where she came from, we would never know.

One day I noticed my husband was out on the deck trying to chase this cat away, to no avail. Finally, he said, "I am going to take her a few blocks down the hill, and maybe she will find her way to her own home." She was wearing a flea collar, so we knew she must belong to someone. My husband remarked, "If she finds her way back here, she has herself a home."

So, he put her in his pickup, and drove a few blocks down the hill, and put her out. Evidently she had made up her mind she was going to live with us, because, by the end of the day the scrawny, dirty looking, little black, and white cat was back. For some unknown reason she was determined to be with us.

My husband made her a bed outside the kitchen door on the deck. He covered the box to make it as warm as possible. It was wintertime, and quite cold. The poor cat was dirty, and had a terrible runny nose. She was just plain "crusty" looking.

After a few days it was apparent she was very ill. I thought she was dying, so decided she should be taken to the "Pound," or taken somewhere to be "put down."

At that time, not being familiar with what procedure I should follow, and too busy to take off and drive the few miles required, I brought her into the kitchen, and made her a bed. By that time she was too weak to stand up and eat. So, I would hold food at her mouth, and she would eat a few bites.

After some time passed, little by little, she gained strength. In the meantime, I told my husband, "It looks like she has "adopted us" so, I am going to name her "Dopper." Thinking back about it, I could have named her a prettier name, but at the time, Dopper seemed to fit.

Dopper was tiny, and easy going, but if a big dog came around, close to the house, she would run them off. She was not afraid of any other cat, or any dog that came around.

Many nights, around midnight, a possum, would come and drink Dopper's water, and eat whatever food had been left on the deck. Dopper would lay in her bed and watch. That was only when she slept outside. Otherwise, she slept in the kitchen with the kitchen doors closed. We kept her in the kitchen because we didn't trust that she wouldn't get sick, and "throw up" on the carpet in the night sometime.

Little by little, without realizing it, I was becoming more and more attached to "Dopper." Every time I sat down she would jump up on my lap. She was happy and content there. If I left the room and she didn't know which way I went, she would go into the hall, look for me, and cry and cry for me.

Since we were somewhat "home-type" people we were seldom gone for very long, except to work. Dopper was with me constantly when I was home. She would lay on my papers when I tried to work, or she was on my lap when I was typing. Or, laying on the dressing table when I was trying to put on make up. If I tried to lie down she either wanted to lay next to my face, or on top of me, to the point of aggravation on my part.

Now, don't get me wrong. She was not one to get on the kitchen or dining room table, or up on the cabinets. Neither was Midnight. That would not have been allowed.

Dopper loved "people food." We made the mistake of feeding her at the dinner table. She would sit between us and stare at us until we would feed her. She would sit indefinitely, persistently, patiently, waiting for us to give her some of our food. She would never give up.

If she didn't get her way she would sit and stare, and give us pitiful, sad looks, like, "How can you treat me this way?" To us, she was funny and adorable.

Sometimes I carried Dopper around like a baby, sometimes we would dance around to the music. I would tell her what a good girl she was. She seemed to be very content as long as I was holding her.

In the morning my husband would be up early, and if he left the kitchen door open she would take off for the bedroom as fast as she could, just crying and crying. She would jump upon the bed, right by my face. She just wanted to be with me.

Without realizing it I was becoming more and more attached to Dopper. She was my baby, my constant companion, and always "there." And, I was her world. At the time I had no idea the effect this would have on me.

Then, one weekend she wasn't eating, and didn't seem to be moving her "bowls." On Monday I took her to the vet. She still appeared to be pretty strong, still walking around and able to jump up on the chair. She was a fighter. I didn't let myself think that she was that ill, and "wouldn't come out of it."

Tuesday, I went to the Vets. Dopper couldn't stand up, she was so weak. She seemed to use all of her strength to try to stand up. We took her into a private room, and she just lay lifeless-like on my lap with her head on my arm.

When I placed her back in the cage she never moved. Early the next morning the Vet called to say Dopper had died in the night.

Unless you are a cat person it is doubtful the average person could understand the loss I felt. After all, she was just a scrawny little cat with a tiny little face. Really not much to look at, although she had put on weight after being with us for awhile. Since I never had children I had let this cat into my heart. It is difficult to express the loss I felt.

For approximately four and a half years she made her home with us. She never ventured very far, a few times across the street. But now, Dopper had left us forever.

She came as a stranger. She chose us, and our home. She captured our hearts. She was a bright light in my life.

Her spirit is alive and well everywhere I look. It is lonely and painful without her. The home is empty without her. The tears continue to fall. Of course, we still have Midnight. I know Midnight misses Dopper something terrible. They often slept together. I think he viewed her as his "cat-sister."

She brought happy, bright days. She brought love. She enriched our lives for four and a half years. Yes, she was very special.

Goodbye, "Dopper." Mamma's good girl. Mamma loves you Baby. Goodbye, Good Girl.

Midnight On Yellow Pillow

"I love to just relax, lay here on this soft, yellow pillow, look at the bears, and Christmas decorations. Hope Santa leaves me some treats in one of those socks."

Midnight and Dopper On Couch And Chair

"Just taking a little nap together. Getting in some "snooze" time. We do that a lot."

MISS DOPPER

AND, THEN THERE WAS DOPPER
SHE'S ADOPTED YOU KNOW
SHE'S OKAY FOR A CAT
AS FAR AS CATS GO.

SHE CAME TO OUR HOUSE
AND, JUST WOULDN'T LEAVE
SHE FOUND AND EASY TOUCH
OR, "SUCKERS," I BELIEVE.

HUSBAND TOOK HER DOWN THE HILL
TOLD HER TO "TAKE A HIKE"
SHE DID—BACK UP THE HILL
HAVE YOU EVER SEEN THE LIKE?

SHE MAY NOT BE THE SMARTEST
BUT, SHE'S PERSISTENT, THAT'S FOR SURE
NO MATTER WHAT HAPPENS
SHE HAS ABILITY TO ENDURE.

AT FIRST SHE WAS ILL
COULDN'T STAND UP TO EAT
BUT, I NURSED HER BACK TO HEALTH
AND, GOT HER BACK ON HER FEET.

SHE JUMPS IN YOUR LAP
EVERY TIME YOU SIT
FOLLOWS FROM ROOM TO ROOM
SHE WON'T GIVE UP, OR QUIT.

SHE LOVES TO BE NEAR YOU
YOU CAN'T KEEP HER OFF YOUR LAP
SHE SNUGGLES ON YOUR TUMMY
IF YOU TRY TO TAKE A NAP.

YOU PUT HER OUTSIDE
TO HAVE A LITTLE PEACE
OTHERWISE, SHE'LL BUG YOU
IT'S THE ONLY WAY SHE'LL CEASE.

SHE CHOSE US FOR HER PARENTS
AND, SHE'S FOUND A HOME, I GUESS
JUST CAUSE SHE'S ADOPTED
WE DON'T LOVE HER ANY LESS.

WHEN YOU TALK ABOUT ADOPTION
I DON'T UNDERSTAND THE FUSS
IT'S A BIT "TURNED AROUND"
MISS DOPPER, ADOPTED US.

Jack, Miss Janet's Cat

"What do you want, Momma? This is my place. Why are you disturbing me?" Can't I get some peace around here?"

JACK, THE ANGEL CAT

This a true story about a cat. Not just any cat. But, perhaps, calling him an "Angel Cat" better describes him. Jack, no doubt, was not his original name, but the name he was given at his new home.

Jack must have run away from his home, or, an Angel decided his presence was needed elsewhere. Or, perhaps, he just got lost and showed up on the doorstep of a very nice couple's home. Janet, the lady of the house, opened the door, and the cat came running in.

Friends of the couple, stopped by at the same time the cat, Jack, appeared. Jack jumped in their laps, frolicked here and there, charming everyone. He loved the petting and attention. They all laughed, and all agreed he was fun, and a beautiful cat.

Everyone was worried about him. They were concerned he had wondered away from his home, and had become lost.

Janet, started asking neighbors if they knew where the adorable cat belonged. She couldn't find anyone to claim him, so she started feeding, and caring for the cat. Janet, and her husband, James, decided to name him, Jack.

Janet took Jack to the Vet to get his shots, and have him checked out.

Jack brought much joy and love into the home, and to James, who was, by then, too ill to get out of bed. Jack would lay for hours by James's side, or at James's feet.

Janet and James felt like a special angel had somehow arranged for Jack to find them. He brought sunshine, and smiles, into the home to help James forget his illness for a bit.

Then, one day, Jack slipped out of the house. Janet and James were very sad. Jack had been such good company, and a diversion for James from his illness.

After Jack had been gone for three days, Janet noticed Jack was sitting out on the back fence. Janet and James were both excited to have Jack's delightful presence back in their home again.

In James' last days, Jack spent most of those days on James' bed. It was as if Jack was watching over James. But, then, when James was gone, Jack seemed lost. He didn't appear to be as happy, and frisky as he had been. Could it be he also went through a grieving period? He seemed no longer his playful self.

It seems Jack was sent to make James' last days a little happier, and more bearable. Jack was a great blessing to Janet, facing lonely days and nights without James.

Yes, surely, Jack was really an "Angel Cat," at least sent by an angel to comfort James in his illness, and Janet in her loss of James.

There are always blessings to count, even in the midst of problems, and losses.

[2] At this writing Jack is still alive, and bringing much joy to my friend, Miss Janet. Jack is not quite as frisky as he used to be at the age he is now. He is, and has been, much company to Miss Janet. She says, "Jack is a good boy," and she is always thankful for her, "Angel Cat, Jack."

Midnight By Kitchen Door

"I sure am hungry. Think I will sneak in the kitchen, and see what I can find to eat. Aren't I a beauty? I am Mr. Big Shot"

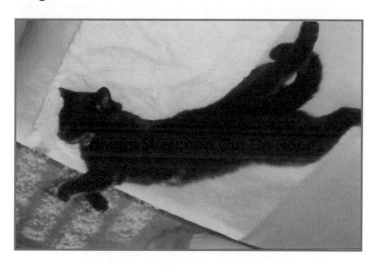

Midnight Stretched Out On Floor

"Just "stretching out" here for awhile, taking it easy. Tired after catching that mouse."

Midnight And Sissy, On Bed

"I tell Sissy, "You stay on your side of the bed, and I'll stay on mine."

Midnight Awakened By Noise, With Sissy Sleeping

"What was that noise? Good thing you didn't wake up my sister, Sissy. She would not be in a good mood!"

Midnight On Pink Bed

"Don't care much for this pink bed. I'm I'm "Mr. Midnight, King of the Hill." I should have a "man pad," not one like this "Girlie pad."

Midnight In Yellow Gold Chair

"I just want to lay here "incognito.""

Pat Holding Midnight By the Tree

"My Momma sure does love me. She likes to show me off. She sure does hold me funny, though."

Pat Holding Midnight In Chair

"I love to sit on my Momma, Pat's lap. I like it when she rubs my back. It makes me purr."

MY NAME IS "MIDNIGHT"

Hi, My name is Midnight. My Master and Mrs. sometimes call me "Mr. Big Shot" or "King of the Hill," 'cause we live up on a hill. Boy, are my parents strange.

I was a Christmas present to my Master from Davey, who is a friend, that lives down the street. Davey rescued me from this big place they call the "Pound." There were lots of homeless cat-children, and parents there. I was happy to be taken away from all that noise and commotion, and happy that Davey rescued me.

Davey sometimes helps my Master with odd jobs around the place. They seem to enjoy spending time together. They are real good friends.

I hope the other homeless cat-children get rescued, and find a home where the parents will love and take care of them. Then, they can have a nice home like mine.

At first I was really scared at my new home. I was just a tiny cat person. I just wanted to get away from everyone, and be by myself.

When Davey brought me to my new home my parents put me out in the garage where there were lots of cabinets, and junk, to hide behind. Then, they brought in this box with funny stuff in it. I had to "go," bad, so I jumped right in the box. My parents laughed, and thought I was cute. They acted surprised that I knew what that box was for. They really are strange.

My Master named me Midnight 'cause I'm all black except for a tiny touch of white under my chin. My parents keep saying things like, "Isn't he cute!"

I've always liked to spend most of my time outside, watching the action. I have to keep an eye on what is going on in the neighborhood. After all, I have to protect my territory.

So, I spend most of my days outside. I find all kind of places to take a nap where no one will bother me. But, after dark, I'd rather be inside with my parents.

My Mrs. tries to feed me all different kinds of "good stuff," but I just eat what I want, when I want. I like my "good stuff" opened fresh, and put in a dish with a separate section for crunchy dry stuff.

If I don't like what she opens all I have to do is fall over on my side, roll around, and she will open a different kind of "good stuff." Guess I am finally getting her trained. Sometimes she is too slow so I jump up on the cabinet, but right away my Mom puts me down. She doesn't allow me to be up on the cabinet. This is my home, so I should be able to do anything I please. I think my Mom has a problem.

When she is putting my food in my dish I stand on my back feet, and slap her robe, or her slacks, with my front paws to get her to hurry up. Or, I play like I am biting her foot or ankle. She doesn't like it much, but she loves me too much to spank me.

My Master can be pretty strict and firm sometimes. But, my Mom is just a "pussy-cat." I don't have to pay attention to her if I don't want to. When she calls, I just ignore her—unless I'm hungry. Then I go in and roll around, and she hurries to get my "good stuff" for me.

My Mom covered over the top of a big chair, and made a place for me to crawl in where it's dark and warm and cozy. They call it my "hidy-hole." If I want to take a nap in the house, and don't want to be disturbed, I just crawl into my "hidy-hole."

Sometimes I jump up on my Moms lap. She pets me and rubs my back. It feels really good, and makes me make a purring sound. I feel warm and safe in my Mom's lap. I know my Mom loves me a lot. I sure am happy I got rescued.

And, my mom has a box that I jump into, and she pulls me around the house. It is fun for me, and she laughs, and thinks it's cute. We have a lot of fun, my mom and me.

One time, when I was a couple of years old, this strange cat-person started coming around. She looked all dirty, and was real sick. My Mom started feeding her, because she felt sorry for her. Then my mom brought her in the house, made her a bed in a basket, and "hand-fed" her in her bed. She couldn't stand up to eat. Little by little she got to feeling better.

My Mom named her "Dopper," 'cause she adopted us. At first I didn't like her invading my territory, but she turned out to be pretty nice—for a girl.

We played a lot, and once in a while Dopper and I would sleep on the big chair, or couch together. Or, we would jump up on the railing off the deck, and check out the view, or watch for birds. But, mostly, I'd rather do my own thing.

When my Mom puts food and water on the deck for Dopper, and me, sometimes other animals come and help themselves. One of those animals my parents call a possum. They take a bite of food, then take a drink. They mess up my water, and get it all dirty. I don't think that is very nice, or friendly.

Dopper uses one of those boxes with the funny stuff in it. Not me. Not anymore. I go out doors where I have privacy. Those boxes are for "sissies,'" and I'm Mr. Big Shot.

But then, one day, Dopper got sick. My parents said they needed to take her to a doctor. But, they came home without her. Everyone was awfully sad, and sometimes I'd see water coming out of my Mom's eyes. Seems like I didn't understand where Dopper had gone, and I really did miss her a lot.

Sometimes my Master and Mrs. sit outside and they act all happy when I come around. I hear them talking, but I just ignore them. I have more important things on my mind, like watching the neighbors, watching for birds, and just laying in the sun, relaxing. I'm pretty busy you know.

Once in a while when I catch a bird, or a mouse, I try to bring them into the house to show them off, but my Mom acts all funny, and makes me play with them outside.

The other day I heard my Master and Mrs. talking. They said they bet I didn't know how lucky I was to have parents who loved me so much. Wonder what they meant by "lucky?"

Well—I have to get going. The neighbor across the street just came home. It's nice and warm under his car. I have a good view from there, and can see in all directions. I've got to keep tabs on what's happening around the neighborhood.

Uh-oh. My parents are calling me. They want me to come in and go "night-night." I'll just ignore them. They should know I am busy checking things out around here. But, they keep calling, "Midnight—come get some "good stuff," and go "night-night."

You know—I wonder if all cat-people have it as rough as me.

Midnight And Dopper On Couch

"Just taking a little nap with my sister, Dopper. I watch out for her, and take care of her."

Midnight And Dopper On Pink Pillow

"Tired out from playing. Getting in a little nap time out here on the deck."

1983

MIDNIGHT

WHO'D EVER HAVE THOUGHT
I COULD FALL FOR A CAT
BUT, WHEN MIDNIGHT CAME ALONG
I WAS "HOOKED," THAT WAS THAT.

HE WILL JUMP IN A BOX
AND, GO FOR A RIDE
WHILE YOU PUSH BACK AND FORTH
OR, SCOOT, SIDE TO SIDE.

HE FALLS ON HIS SIDE
AND THEN DOES A FLOP
HE JUMPS ON THE BED
AND, JUST GOES "KER-PLOP."

WHEN YOU DRIVE IN THE GARAGE
HE JUMPS ON THE CAR
CLIMBS IN THE WINDOW
TO BE WHERE YOU ARE.

HE'S SHINY AND BLACK
A SPOT OF WHITE ON HIS THROAT
SO SOFT TO THE TOUCH
OF HIS BEAUTIFUL "COAT."

HE CURLS UP IN A BALL
AND, SOMETIMES HE PURRS
WAKES US UP AT FOUR A.M.
THIS OFTEN OCCURS.

HE CUDDLES REAL CLOSE
TO YOUR SIDE IN THE BED
SEEMS TO UNDERSTAND
WHATEVER YOU SAID.

HE LAYS ON YOUR LEGS
MEOWS FOR SOME FOOD
NUDGES YOU WITH HIS NOSE
IN A PLAYFUL MOOD.

YOU MENTION "OUTSIDE"
HE HEADS FOR THE DOOR
WITH MIDNIGHT AROUND
LIFE IS NEVER A BORE.

HE REALLY IS UNUSUAL
AND, EVER SO SMART
THERE IS ONLY ONE "MIDNIGHT"
HE HAS CAPTURED MY HEART.

Midnight In Box

"I love it when my Mom pulls me around in a box. We have a lot of fun. She just laughs and laughs. Then, I just fall over, and rest for awhile."

Midnight On Pillow

"I am really tired waiting here for Santa. Found me another soft pillow. Guess Mr. Clown will let me know when Santa gets here. He looks wide awake."

Midnight On Porch Rail

"Waiting up here to see what's gonna happen next. I might even see a bird to chase."

Midnight and Sissy on Porch Rail

"Just hanging out here with my Sister, Sissy. We keep tabs on what is going on in the neighborhood."

5/17/1997

MR. MIDNIGHT

DEAR, PRECIOUS MIDNIGHT, TODAY'S THE DAY
WE MUST HAVE YOU "PUT AWAY."

PUT TO SLEEP, OUR TEARS ARE FLOWING
OH THE PAIN, TO KNOW YOU'RE "GOING."

YOU STILL LOOK UP, AND MOVE YOUR TAIL
BUT, YOU'VE BECOME SO THIN, AND FRAIL.

YOU WON'T DRINK WATER, OR EVEN EAT
TOO WEAK TO STAND UP ON YOUR FEET.

YOU'VE BEEN OUR SPECIAL "MIDNIGHT-CHILD"
WE LOVE YOU SO, THAT'S PUTTING IT MILD.

SIXTEEN YEARS, YOU'VE BEEN OUR JOY
"KING OF THE HILL," OUR "MIDNIGHT BOY."

NO ONE WILL EVER TAKE YOUR PLACE
DAYS WITHOUT YOU WILL BE HARD TO FACE.

PLEASE FORGIVE US FOR ALL THE "FUSS"
WE'RE JUST FEELING SORRY—FOR US.

==

NOW, LIFE WILL NEVER BE THE SAME
"BIG SHOT, MIDNIGHT," WAS HIS NAME.

Miss Priscilla And Puppy

"I'm glad I'm grown up, and don't play in the leaves. I don't think that puppy will find anything to eat down there."

Prissy Sitting Up For Pat

"My Mom likes me to sit up for my treats. She thinks I am beautiful and smart."

Prissy On chain

"Don't leave me out here. I want to be with you."

Pat With Cocker Puppy

"Am I not the cutest thing? My Mom thinks so."

MISS PRISCILLA

Miss Priscilla. Nickname, "Prissy." Perfect name. Blonde. Shaggy ears. Cocker Spaniel. Beautiful. Smart. So smart.

When you heard the word "go," you would always run to the door. Anxious. You were always ready to go.

You were always happy to be with me. One time you took a road trip with me to Texas to visit relatives. A few years later you took a long road trip with me over the ALCAN Highway, to Anchorage, Alaska, where we stayed for awhile.

Neither of us were fond of the cold, but, being young, we managed. When it was cold, and snow on the ground, (which was much of the time,) you would run outside, potty, and quickly, run right back into the house. You were so cute and funny.

When I came home from work, or after being away from the house, you would always be standing, looking out the window, waiting for me, watching me drive into the driveway. You were always there, happy, excited, wagging your tail.

Then, you took a plane ride. First from Anchorage to Seattle, Washington, then, from Seattle to Oakland, California. For a little dog, you did get around.

You were like a child to me. My baby. When you had your own puppy, it was born dead. You only had one. You grieved that your baby didn't live. You cried and cried. You wouldn't stop crying. We finally got a doll-toy, and put it in your bed. You finally stopped crying.

After six, happy, fun, memorable years, you went to Doggie Heaven. My Miss Priscilla. My Prissy Baby. A terrible, sad, loss. But, you gave enormous joy for all those years. For that, I will always be thankful.

9/4/2010

MISSY

MISSY, SWEET MISSY-CAT
KITTY HEAVEN OPENED IT'S DOOR
AT TWO FORTY NINE A. M.
YOUR PRESENCE, WITH US NO MORE.

NO LONGER ABLE TO EAT
AS WEAKER YOU BECAME
OLD AGE PLAYED A PART
OUR DAYS, NEVER THE SAME.

SUCH A LOVING KITTY
TO BE HELD, YOUR CONSTANT DESIRE
IN OUR HANDS, OR ARMS
YOU SEEM TO NEVER TIRE.

MANY YEARS IN THE "ELEMENTS"
SUMMERS AND WINTERS, OUTSIDE
UNTIL I MADE YOU A "HOUSE CAT"
UNTIL THE DAY YOU DIED.

TEARS NOW FILL OUR EYES
IN SADNESS WE ARE "CLAD"
THAT YOU ARE NOT IN PAIN
FOR THIS, WE'RE THANKFUL, AND GLAD.

YOU FILLED OUR LIVES WITH JOY
ALWAYS BRIGHTENED OUR DAYS
GONE, BUT NOT FORGOTTEN
YOU'LL REMAIN IN OUR HEARTS, ALWAYS.

Annie And Chrissy Laying On Floor

"Fun just to snuggle up, and take a nap."

Annie Walking On Rug. Chrissy Laying Down

"Think I will just take a walk. I'm tired of just laying around all the time. I want to check things out, outside."

Chrissy And Annie On Top Concrete Step

"We really enjoy the warm, sunshine. The step is nice and warm. I love spending time with my sister. We have a lot of fun."

Chrissy On Bottom Step

"Just love relaxing, looking around, on this warm step, watching what goes on in the neighborhood."

Chrissy And Annie On Bed

"Why did you bother us with that camera? We weren't bothering anybody. Can't we take a nap in peace?"

Chrissy And Annie On Gold Frame Bed

"Can't you see we are taking a nap? We need our "beauty sleep.".

MY CHRISSY-CAT

MY CHRISSY BABY, TEARS FILL MY EYES.
THE HURT FROM LOSING YOU, I CAN'T DISGUISE.

MY CHRISSY-KITTY, IT SADDENS ME SO
THAT IT WAS YOUR TIME, YOUR TIME TO GO.

NO MORE SUFFERING, NOW, NO MORE PAIN
BUT, FROM TEARS, I CANT REFRAIN.

I TRY TO THINK IT IS FOR YOUR OWN GOOD
SO MANY LOSSES, NOT ALWAYS UNDERSTOOD.

BUT, LIFE GOES ON, SOMEHOW, SOME WAY
WITHOUT YOU HERE, I HAVE TO GET THROUGH THE DAY.

I AM SO SAD, I CAN NOT PRETEND
BUT, THANKFUL YOUR SUFFERING HAS COME TO AN END.

THOUGH YOU WERE WILD WHEN YOU CAME TO US
YOU SOON BECAME TAME, AND MADE NO FUSS.

IN THE END, YOU WENT BLIND, COULDN'T SEE
FROM YOUR BLINDNESS, NOW YOU ARE FREE.

HERE NOW, THIS HOME, NEVER THE SAME
MY HEART IS ACHING, CRYING OUT YOUR NAME.

I'M THANKFUL FOR ALL THE JOY YOU GAVE
WITH YOU, YOUR PINK HONEY BEAR, WILL LIE IN YOUR GRAVE.

IN "KITTY HEAVEN" YOU ARE NOW AT PEACE
MY LOVE FOR YOU WILL NEVER CEASE

Annie, Out And About

"I'm just "out and about," checking things out."

Annie, With Chrissy On Bed

"We are trying to get some sleep. Why do you keep taking our picture? At least give us time to "pose."

Annie On Yellow Chair

"I like this bright, colorful, wicker chair. It's one of my favorite places to relax."

Annie, In Bedding

"Hope I don't lose my sister in here. Well, she was here, somewhere, awhile ago. Love these really soft blankets to take my nap, or to jump around, and have fun in."

Annie And Sammy On Bed

"We're trying to get some sleep. You keep taking our picture. You must think we're special."

Annie and Sammy Hanging Out On Bed

"Just hanging out here together! Taking it easy."

MY DEAREST ANNIE-CAT

FRIDAY EVENING YOUR SPIRIT FLEW AWAY
TOO WEAK TO GET UP, EAT, RUN, AND PLAY.

YOU'RE MY LAST KITTY CAT-CHILD TO "GO"
THINGS WON'T BE THE SAME, I MISS YOU SO.

YOU JOINED DOPPER, MIDNIGHT, SISSY, AND CHRISSY
AND, MY FIRST AND ONLY DOG, MISS PRISCILLA, "PRISSY."

FOR ANY LOSS YOU CAN NEVER PREPARE
FOR AWHILE, THE LOSS IS SO HARD TO BEAR.

BUT, LIFE GOES ON, WITH PROBLEMS TO CONFRONT
FROM DIFFICULTIES, YOU "BEAR THE BRUNT."

I THANK YOU FOR THE YEARS YOU BROUGHT JOY
I WADDED UP PIECES OF PAPER, THAT WAS YOUR "TOY."

BATTING THE PAPER, WITH YOUR FRONT PAW, ACROSS THE FLOOR
THEN, TOSSING IT UP, YOU WERE NEVER A BORE.

THE LAST DAY YOUR STRENGTH BEGAN TO "WANE"
ALTHOUGH YOU DIDN'T APPEAR TO BE IN ANY PAIN.

I HELD YOU CLOSE, YOU LAY VERY STILL
I DIDN'T WANT TO FACE THAT YOUR "GOING" WAS REAL.

NOW IN "KITTY HEAVEN," FOREVER TO REST
ANNIE, MY ANNIE-CAT, YOU WERE THE "BEST."

Sammy Under Cover Of Umbrella

"Love my umbrella. No sunburn for me today. Sun, rain, sleet, or snow, will not get to me."

Sammy With Toy

"Just minding my own business, playing with my toy."

Sammy With Electric Collar

"Why do they put this contraption around my neck? I won't run away again, I promise."

Sammy Getting Ready To Take A Nap

"I am really tired, and this place is really comfortable. Great place for a nap."

Sammy Resting On Backhoe

"I'm just laying here trying to figure out how to get this backhoe started, so I can take a little ride."

OUR SAMMY-DOG

OUR PRECIOUS SAMMY-DOG
ON THIS RAINY, DISMAL DAY
WE MUST HAVE YOU PUT TO SLEEP
FOREVER FROM US--AWAY .

YOU'VE BEEN LIKE OUR CHILD
LOVED MORE THAN YOU COULD KNOW
WE'VE CRIED ENDLESS TEARS
IT'S SO HARD TO LET YOU GO.

ONLY EIGHT YEARS OLD
YOU'VE BEEN OUR PRIDE AND JOY
THE SWEETEST PERSONALITY
OUR PRECIOUS SAMMY, BOY

DISEASE CALLED LYMPHOMA
A TERRIBLE WAY TO DIE
WE DON'T WANT YOU TO SUFFER
IT'S JUST SO HARD TO SAY GOOD BYE.

PRETTY BLONDE IN COLOR
WE THINK YOU'RE SO SMART
EASILY LEARNING TRICKS
YOU CAPTURED OUR HEART.

THIS FIRST DAY OF OCTOBER
WE FEEL OUR HEARTS WILL BREAK
THAT WE MUST GIVE YOU UP
IT'S JUST SO HARD TO TAKE.

————————————————————————

THE VET CAME TO THE CAR
AND GAVE YOU A SHOT
PUTTING YOU TO SLEEP
RIGHT THERE ON THE SPOT.

NOW ROAMING AROUND DOG HEAVEN
NOW YOU'RE FREE AT LAST
ROLLING OVER FOR YOUR TREATS
DANCING ON TWO FEET REAL FAST.

HOPE THEY SERVE YOU ICE CREAM
WHEN THEY OPEN THE FREEZER DOOR
YOU'LL BE RIGHT THERE WAITING
SAYING, "JUST A LITTLE MORE."

THEY DON'T COME ANY SMARTER
WE KNOW WE'VE HAD THE BEST
FOREVER IN OUR MEMORY
OUR LIVES, WITH SAMMY--BLESSED.

8/22/91

RAIDER

DEAR MR. RAIDER-DOG
WHAT A SPECIAL "GUY"
ON HEARING OF YOUR "PASSING"
I COULDN'T HELP BUT CRY.

YOU BRIGHTENED RICKY'S LIFE
ALWAYS BY HIS SIDE
"JUMPING" IN THE CAR
ANXIOUS TO GO FOR A RIDE.

NAMED AFTER THE "RAIDERS"
WHO COULD HAVE EVER GUESSED
HOW MUCH YOU'D MEAN TO RICK
HOW MUCH HIS LIFE WOULD BE BLESSED.

DISCIPLINED BY RICK'S MOM
MARIE, --SHE LOVED YOU TOO
SHE WOULD "LOOK AFTER YOU"
WHEN RICK HAD THINGS TO DO.

YOU WOULD COME TO GREET US
HAPPILY WAVING YOUR TAIL
YOU'D COME AROUND FOR SOME PETTING
ALMOST WITHOUT FAIL.

NOW THERE'LL BE A VOID
--NEVER AGAIN THE SAME
BUT YOU'VE GONE TO A "BETTER PLACE"
TO "DOG HEAVEN"--YOUR FAME TO CLAIM.

YOU WERE A GREAT COMPANION
ONE RICK WILL NEVER FORGET
"FLUFFY," HANDSOME, AND PROUD
A "ONE OF A KIND," LOVING PET.

[3] Ricky was a friend of Carol and Al Davis, who owned the Raider Football Team. That is how Raider-Dog got his name. Pat wrote this poem for Ricky after Raider died.

RUSH'S "PUNKIN"

PUNKIN--MY SWEET PUNKIN
STOP "BUTT-HEADING" ME
I'VE GOT TO GET SOME SLEEP
I'M TIRED AS I CAN BE.

PUNKIN--I LOVE YOU
BUT--PLEASE GO TAKE A NAP
IN JUST A FEW HOURS
I MUST "PUT ON MY THINKING CAP."

O PUNKIN--YOU SPOILED KITTY
I DO LOVE YOU SO
IN JUST A FEW HOURS
I GO ON THE RADIO.

I KNOW YOU RUN THE HOUSE
YOU'RE FINICKY WITH YOUR FOOD
IF YOU DON'T GET WHAT YOU WANT
YOU'RE IN A VERY BAD MOOD.

I MAKE UP DIFFERENT "BAGGIES"
TO FIND THE ONE YOU'LL EAT
PUNKIN--LEAVE ME ALONE
STOP "KNEADING" ME WITH YOUR FEET.

PUNKIN--COME ON PUNKIN
FROM YOUR "BUTT-HEADING," PLEASE REFRAIN
IT'S A GOOD THING FOR MY SHOW
IT ONLY REQUIRES "HALF MY BRAIN."

PUNKIN--MY DEAR PUNKIN
I PROMISE I'LL PLAY WITH YOU LATER
JUST LET ME GET SOME SLEEP
THEN TO ALL YOUR DEMANDS I'LL "CATER."

MY DEAR PUNKIN, IT'S UP TO ME
TO MAKE MY PROGRAM GREAT
"TALENT ON LOAN FROM GOD"
I'M NOT GOING TO MAKE THEM WAIT.

[4] Pat wrote this poem after listening to Rush Limbaugh, on the radio, talk about his kitty-cat, Punkin

10/21/2018

Don's Chloe, Sheltie Sheep Dog

"Am I not fantastic looking? My Dad, Don, brushes me every day. He likes to show me off."

WAGON TAILS TO YOU

WE ARE SHELTIE DOGS
BEAUTIFULLY BORN AND BRED
OUR MASTER'S PRIDE AND JOY
WITH SPECIAL ATTENTION-- FED.

WE GO TO OBEDIENT SCHOOL
TO MAKE OUR OWNER'S PROUD
WE DO ALL KINDS OF TRICKS
THAT DELIGHT, AND EXCITE THE CROWD.

THEY LOVE TO SHOW US OFF
WITH OUR COATS SHINY AND BRIGHT
THEY SPEND LOTS OF TIME WITH US
PAMPERING US, DAY AND NIGHT.

"DOG PEOPLE" ARE DIFFERENT
A DIFFERENT "BREED" ALL THEIR OWN
WE GET LOTS OF "GOODIES"
AT TIMES, A "DELECTABLE BONE."

NOW--"WAGON TAILS TO YOU"
HOPE SOON AGAIN WE'LL MEET
TO SHOW OFF FOR OUR MASTER'S
AND FOR US—A "TASTY TREAT."

[5] Pat wrote this for a Sheltie Dog Show in Colorado.

MoJo and MaJor, Peggy And Billy Wiggens, "Children"

"Just me and my brother, "hanging out together." "Aren't we a couple of good-looking dudes?"

MaJor Wiggins With Book

"Reading my book just "wore me out." Guess I'll catch a little "shut-eye."

MaJor And MoJo With Hats

"We love our hats. Real stylish, huh?"

MaJor With Toy

"That was a lot of fun playing with this toy. I think it got the best of me. I'm too tired to get up."

Don And Pat With Scoobie

"My Aunt Pat sure is holding me funny. She just wants to show me off."

Jerry With Star And Scoobie

"Our Dad, Jerry, thinks we are beautiful. He likes to "show us off." We love it when he takes us to the doggie-park to play. I go up to him every afternoon, and stare, and look at him with my begging eyes until he takes Star and me to the doggie-park. We can run and play there, and have a good time."

Cassie And Star

"Aren't we cute? Our parents, Jerry and Sondra, think we are just the cutest, and they love us a lot."

Cassie With Scarf

"I just got all groomed, and "beautified. How do you like my scarf?"

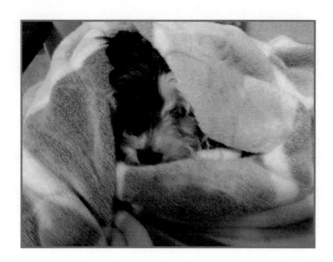

Scoobie After Bath

"I don't know why I have to have a bath. My dad says I "smell," whatever that means. I just want to snuggle up here in this towel, get warm, and be left alone."

Pearl And Friend

"Strange playmate. That moose is just trying to "outshine" me, but I'm prettier than him."

Jerry Aggravating Pearl

"My dad, Jerry, aggravates me, and I pretend I am really mad at him. Sometimes he thinks I am having a panic attack."

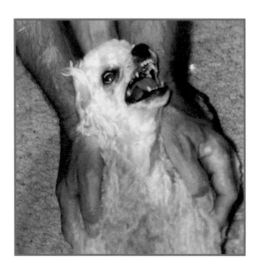

Pearl, Being Teased, Snarling At Jerry

"Showing my dentures when my Dad, Jerry, teases me. Yikes, Dad. Enough fun for today."

Pearl With Pink Bows

"See how pretty I am when my Dad, Jerry, isn't teasing me. I love all the pink bows."

Sondra, With Star Wearing Santa Hat

"That's my Mom, Sondra, holding me. She thinks I'm adorable, and she loves me a lot. She's in the "Christmas Spirit," showing me off in my Santa Hat."

Star Baby

"Aren't I cute. I was just a baby when my Momma and Daddy, Sondra and Jerry, got me. They take really good care of me. They keep me groomed all beautiful."

Star Licking Her Chops

"That sure was yummy food. Bet you can't stick your tongue out this far."

Meagan With Star And Scoobie-Doo

"Miss Meagan showing me and Scoobie off. Meagan is the Granddaughter of my parents, Sondra and Jerry. Meagan is a big "Star," softball player. Oh, "Star," that is my name too, I'm here with my sister, Scoobie-Doo."

Sissy Sitting On Top Of Chair

"Just relaxing here on top of this big chair. It's comfortable, and easier to check things out."

Sissy Laying On Floor

"Love to just lay here on the floor, and relax. My Mom, Pat, loves me a lot, and lets me, pretty much, "Have the run of the house.""

Sissy On Green Chair

"Here I am again on my Mom's green chair. My favorite place to day dream."

Sissy Laying On Green Towel

"Just trying to get some "shut eye." How come you're always taking my picture?"

Pat Holding Sissy By Tree

"That's my Mom, Miss Pat, holding me, and showing off her Christmas Tree." She likes to put up all kinds of fancy stuff for Christmas."

Sissy On Green Chair

"Laying here on this green chair. I like my Mom's lap better."

Pat Petting Sissy By Tree

"Here I am laying on my Momma, Pat's, lap again. It's my favorite place. It's warm and cozy, and I know she loves me. She really likes petting me, and it feels so good."

Sissy And Midnight On Towel On Bed

"Here with my brother, Midnight. Just curled up, catching a little "shut eye. We do this a lot."

Miss Pat, By Tree, Holding Sissy

"I love to lay on my Mom's lap. I like her holding me. Makes me feel loved, warm, and secure. She rubs my back too. Makes me sleepy."

Sissy On Barney's Lap

"Here I am laying on Barney's lap, but someone doesn't know how to take pictures. They cut off poor Barney's head."

Pat And Sammy By Fireplace

"Guess my Mom, Pat, likes to show me off. She thinks I'm handsome, and smart. I like to do tricks for her. She has me sit, and throws me my treats, and I catch them. And, I can dance. I can dance round on my two hind legs. I really can. My Dad, Don, taught me."

A - B - C'S OF THE BIBLE

A - IS FOR ADAM
THE FIRST MAN GOD MADE
IN THE GARDEN OF EDEN
HE SINNED AND DISOBEYED.

B - IS FOR THE BIBLE
GOD'S WORD FOR ME AND YOU
IT CONTAINS SIXTY SIX BOOKS
IN TWO PARTS--OLD AND NEW.

C - IS FOR CHRIST
AND THE CROSS WHERE HE DIED
FOR THE SINS OF THE WORLD
OUR LORD WAS CRUCIFIED.

D - IS FOR DANIEL
PLACED IN THE LION'S DEN
BUT, HIS LIFE WAS SPARED
HE WAS FOUND WITH OUT SIN.

E - IS FOR EVE
CREATED AS ADAM'S MATE
THEY WERE TEMPTED BY THE DEVIL
THEN, OF THE FORBIDDEN FRUIT, THEY ATE.

F - IS FOR FAITH
FAITH IN GOD'S POWER
THAT FROM A TINY SEED
CAN GROW A BEAUTIFUL FLOWER.

G - IS FOR GOD
WHO CREATED YOU AND ME
HE GAVE HIS ONLY SON'
THAT FROM SIN WE'D BE SET FREE.

H - IS FOR HANNAH
WHO HAD NO SON
BUT, SHE PRAYED TO GOD
AND HE GAVE HER ONE.

I - IS FOR ISAAC
THE SON OF ABRAHAM
WHO WAS SPARED ON THE ALTER
GOD ACCEPTING INSTEAD--A RAM.

J - IS FOR JOB
WHO GOD PUT THROUGH A TEST
BUT, BECAUSE OF JOB'S FAITH
IN THE END, WAS GREATLY BLESSED.

K - IS FOR KINDNESS
SHOW OTHERS YOU CARE
TREAT YOUR NEIGHBOR AS YOURSELF
AND, SPREAD KINDNESS EVERYWHERE.

L - IS FOR LOVE
LOVE FOR GOD'S SON
LOVE FOR LIFE
AND, LOVE FOR EVERY ONE.

M - IS FOR MARY
TO WHOM JESUS WAS BORN
WISE MEN CAME FROM FAR AND NEAR
THE CHILD TO ADORN.

N - IS FOR NOAH
WHO BUILT AN ARK OF WOOD
GOD SAVED HIM FROM THE FLOOD
BECAUSE HE WAS GOOD.

O - IS FOR OBEY
OBEY GOD'S WORD
PRAISE HIS HOLY NAME
AND, YOUR VOICE WILL BE HEARD.

P - IS FOR PRAYER
PRAY FOR YOUR DAILY BREAD
ASK AND HE WILL GIVE YOU
A PLACE TO LAY YOUR HEAD.

Q - IS FOR QUIET
TAKE TIME EACH DAY
TO SPEND QUIET TIME WITH GOD
A QUIET TIME TO PRAY.

R - IS FOR RUTH
WHO GLEANED FOR WHEAT IN BOAZ'S FIELD
HE PURCHASED HER HAND FROM HIS KINSMAN
AND WITH HIS SHOE--THE BARGAIN WAS SEALED.

S - IS FOR SOLOMON
THE WISEST MAN OF HIS DAY
HE BUILT A HOUSE FOR THE LORD
BUT, THEN HIS HEART WAS TURNED AWAY.

T - IS FOR THOMAS
WHO TOUCHED THE HOLES IN JESUS' SIDE
HE DOUBTED THE LORD HAD RISEN
AFTER OUR LORD WAS CRUCIFIED.

U - IS FOR UNSELFISH
WE SHOULD CHEERFULLY GIVE
OUR LOVE, OUR TIME, OUR TALENTS
AND FOR CHRIST, UNSELFISHLY LIVE.

V - IS FOR THE VIRGIN
SHE GAVE BIRTH TO A SON
BUT, HE DIED ON THE CROSS
FOR THE SINS OF EVERYONE.

W - IS FOR WORSHIP
AS WE'RE COMMANDED TO DO
WHERE A FEW ARE JOINED TOGETHER
THE LORD WILL BE THERE, TOO.

X - AS IN CRUCIFIXION
JESUS NAILED TO THE CROSS TO DIE
"MY GOD, WHY HAST THOU FORSAKEN ME?"
IN ANGUISH, HE DID CRY.

Y - IS FOR YOU
THROUGH LOVE YOU WERE MADE
YOU ARE GOD'S CHILD
"BE NOT AFRAID"

Z - IS FOR ZION
WE LONG THY GATES TO SEE
WHERE OUR HEAVENLY FATHER AWAITS
WITH OPEN ARMS--FOR YOU AND ME.

BEE-WARE

MR. BUMBLE BEE
YOU BEST BEE-HAVE
OR, I WILL SEND YOU
TO AN EARLY GRAVE.

AND, IF YOU THINK
I'M NOT ALERT
YOU ARE GONNA' BE
IN A "WORLD OF HURT."

SO, DON'T "BUG" ME
AND, YOU, I'LL IGNORE
BUT, BUZZ MY FACE
AND YOU'RE ON THE FLOOR.

SO, GO "DO YOUR THING"
AND, GO "POLLINATE"
AND NEITHER OF US WILL WORRY
ABOUT YOUR FATE.

EVERY DAY IS "FUN DAY"

EVERY DAY IS "FUN DAY" AT THE FAIR
MANY DIFFERENT ACTIVITIES HAPPENING THERE.

EXCITEMENT FOR ALL AGES, EVERYONE
HURRY TO THE FAIR, AND HAVE SOME FUN.

VIEW THE NUMEROUS EXHIBITS DISPLAYED WITH PRIDE
JUMP ON THE FERRIS WHEEL, AND TAKE A RIDE.

THERE'LL BE "CLOWNING AROUND," AND GOODIES GALORE
INVITE YOUR NEIGHBORS AND FRIENDS—DON'T BE A BORE.

COMPETE FOR RIBBONS, 1ST AND 2ND PLACE
OR, STOP BY, AND SEE THE HORSES RACE.

CHECK THE FINE ARTS, THE LANDSCAPE DESIGN
SEE SHEEP, GOATS, AND HORSES, AND SWINE.

QUILTING, PHOTOGRAPHY, FANCY CAKES
RIBBONS, AND MONEY, THE WINNER TAKES.

CREATIVITY, AND EXCELLENCE—THERE TO VIEW
ENTERTAINMENT, WITH ENDLESS THINGS TO DO.

SIXTEEN GREAT, FUN, DAYS—COME ONE, COME ALL
PARTICIPATE, MAKE MEMORIES, HAVE A BALL.

1983

ME AND MY "TENNIE'S"

JUST ME AND MY "TENNIE'S"
WE WALK ALONG
WITH A SWING IN OUR STEP
MOVING ON, SINGING A SONG.

WE CAN JUMP REAL HIGH
OR, TAKE A BIG STEP
WITH TENNIE'S ON MY FEET
I'VE GOT LOTS OF PEP.

THEY GET ME CROSS COUNTRY
OR, TO THE OLE FISHING HOLE
AND, WE KEEP ON A WALKING
IT'S GOOD FOR THE SOUL.

WE CAN KICK A BALL
EVEN RUN A RACE
GET FROM HERE TO THERE
AND, TO SOME OTHER PLACE.

ME AND MY TENNIE'S
WE HARDLY FEEL A BUMP
MUCH MORE COMFORTABLE
THAN A SANDAL, OR A PUMP.

MY NAME-BRAND TENNIE'S
WE'VE GOT LOTS OF FRIENDS
WHEN I LOOK AROUND
I SEE A LOT OF TWINS.

LOVE MY TENNIE'S
WE STAY ON THE GO
I'LL KEEP WEAR MY TENNIE'S
WHILE STILL LIVING HERE, "BELOW."

ROAD KILL CAFE

DOWN AT THE ROAD KILL CAFE
ENJOY THE ROAD KILL OF THE DAY.

WE HAVE SKUNK--BLACK OR WHITE
WOULD YOU CARE TO TRY A BITE?

A LEG OF RABBIT, GIVE IT A WHIRL
OR, WOULD YOU PREFER, BREAST OF SQUIRREL?

A SUPERB SAMPLING OF RATTLESNAKE
FOR DESERT, SOME COW PIE, OR WARM CAKE.

A GLASS OF BUG JUICE TO WASH IT DOWN
DID I CATCH ON YOUR FACE A FROWN?

ARMADILLO STEAKS--FRESH TODAY
LOTS OF TREATS, TRAVELING LIFE'S HIGHWAY.

WE HAVE SOME SPECIAL, TASTY, RACCOON STEW
OR, TRY OUR TURTLE SOUP, BEFORE YOU'RE THROUGH.

WE'RE ALWAYS HAPPY TO ACCOMMODATE
FOR THIS EXPERIENCE—YOU DON'T WANT TO WAIT.

THE ROAD KILL CAFE IS HERE TO SERVE
JUST HELP YOURSELF TO "ONE MORE HORS D'OEUVRE."

[6] When Pat and Don were traveling through Texas in their RV, Coach, Pat saw a sign that said, "Road Kill Cafe." She couldn't believe her eyes. They both laughed about the sign. Pat immediately wrote this poem.

THE BLACK SNAKE

SHE WALKED OUT TO THE FRONT PORCH
TO GET A BREATH OF FRESH AIR
SHE NEVER COULD HAVE IMAGINED
WHAT AWAITED HER THERE.

WALKING AROUND TO THE SIDE
TO WATCH HER HUSBAND WORKING
SHE HAD NO WAY OF KNOWING
WHAT, AT HER FEET, WAS "LURKING."

AS SHE GLIMPSED DOWNWARD
THERE BEFORE HER FRIGHTENED EYES
SOMETHING VERY UNEXPECTED
WAS, FOR HER, A BIG SURPRISE.

LAYING THERE ON THE PORCH
JUST BESIDE HER FEET
A LONG, BLACK SNAKE
SEEMINGLY, THERE TO GREET.

WITHOUT ANY HESITATION
FOR HER HUSBAND, SHE CALLED
TO SEE THIS SNAKE ON THE PORCH
SHE WAS NOT "ENTHRALLED."

HER HUSBAND HEARD HER CALL
RUSHED TO HIS WIFE'S SIDE
CAREFULLY PICKED UP THE SNAKE
CARRIED IT AWAY, WITH PRIDE.

HE TOOK IT OUT A WAYS
CALMLY LAID IT BY A TREE
ALLOWED IT TO LIVE ANOTHER DAY
HE SET THAT BLACK SNAKE "FREE."

BLACK SNAKES ARE NOT DANGEROUS
THAT IS WHAT WE'VE BEEN TOLD
BUT, TO PICK ONE UP, AND CARRY IT
SHE WOULD NEVER HAVE BEEN THAT BOLD.

BUT, BRAVERY BY HER HUSBAND
ON THAT BRIGHT, SUNNY DAY
SAVED HER FROM THAT BLACK SNAKE
HER FOREVER HERO, HE WOULD STAY.

[7] This is a true story. Pat walked out on the side porch of their home, looked down, and saw the snake at her feet.

THE BUG

I SAW THIS BUG, LAYING "UPSIDE DOWN"
I SAID, "THAT'S WHAT HAPPENED TO ME"
I SAW THIS BUG—STRUGGLING THERE
HOPING, SOMEHOW, TO GET "FREE."

I FLIPPED THAT BUG BACK ON IT'S FEET
SO, IT COULD GO ON IT'S WAY
I WONDER IF IT UNDERSTOOD
I SAVED IT'S LIFE TODAY.

IT CRAWLED AWAY—TO DO IT'S THING
WHATEVER IT IS BUGS DO
SAVED FROM AN IMMEDIATE "PROBLEM"
I WAS ABLE TO "HELP IT THROUGH."

WE NEVER KNOW HOW WE MAY HELP
SOME STRUGGLING SOUL WE MEET
PERHAPS, LIFTING THEM UP
AND, GETTING THEM "BACK ON THEIR FEET."

WITH MY PROPERTIES, I GOT "UPSIDE DOWN"
WHEN THE REAL ESTATE MARKET FELL
RESULTING IN QUITE A LOSS
A TRAGIC STORY TO TELL.

SO, IF YOU SEE SOMEONE IN TROUBLE
AND, HEAR THEIR MOURNFUL PLEA
DON'T JUST PASS THEM BY, OR SAY
DON'T COME AROUND "BUGGING ME."

BUT, OFFER TO LEND A HELPING HAND
AS YOU'D HOPE THEY'D DO FOR YOU
AND, THE WORLD WILL BE A BETTER PLACE
FOR US ALL, AS WE PASS THROUGH.

[8] One day Pat was sitting at her desk, and she saw a bug laying there upside down, struggling. She turned it right side up, and it went on it's way.

In the 1990's, in a "down" real estate market in California, Pat ended up losing a number of rental properties—thus the "inspiration" for the poem.

THE PIGEON'S FLIGHT

I SAT AND WATCHED A FLOCK OF PIGEONS
FLYING THROUGH THE AIR
SO INTRIGUING, AND SO BEAUTIFUL
ALL I COULD DO WAS STARE.

ROUND AND ROUND AND ROUND THEY WENT
CUTTING THROUGH THE BREEZE
THEY'D FLAP THEIR WINGS--THEN SOAR A BIT
WITH--OH SUCH GRACE AND EASE.

ROUND AND ROUND AND ROUND THEY SOARED
TO THE LEFT--THEN TO THE RIGHT
OUT FOR THEIR MORNING EXERCISE
TAKING THEIR MORNING FLIGHT.

THE OTHER BIRDS WOULD SCATTER
AS THE PIGEONS MADE THEIR WAY
UP, AND AROUND, AND OVER, THEY WENT
WHAT A START OF A BEAUTIFUL DAY.

THEN, LOWER AND LOWER, THEY CIRCLED
SOME RETURNING TO THEIR NEST
THEN, AFTER A FEW MORE ROUNDS
THE LAST FIVE JOINED THE REST.

WHAT A BEAUTIFUL WAY TO START THE DAY
WHAT A GLORIOUS SIGHT TO SEE
ANOTHER MIRACLE FROM GOD
THE SAME AS YOU, AND ME.

[9] Pat, sitting, looking out her living room window, down below, she watched, while a flock of pigeons "did their thing."

Dogwood Tree, And Don's Shop

"Beautiful Dogwood Tree, and shop, where Don spends most of his time."

THE DOGWOOD

THE ELEGANT DOGWOOD TREE
EACH YEAR IN EARLY SPRING
BRINGS FORTH COLORFUL BLOSSOMS
MUCH BEAUTY, ON EARTH, TO BRING.

SPRINKLED THROUGH OUT THE LANDSCAPE
INTERMINGLED, MAJESTIC, AND PROUD
DRESSED UP IN IT'S SPLENDOR
WITH SPECTACULAR COLORS, ENDOWED.

SCATTERED BETWEEN PINE AND OAK
BRILLIANT PINK, WHITE, AND RED
GOD'S WONDROUS CREATION
WITH BREATHTAKING SCENES, WE'RE "FED."

I HEARD ABOUT THIS LEGEND
ABOUT A LARGE DOGWOOD TREE
IT'S WOOD FIRM AND STRONG
USED AS A "CROSS" AT CALVARY.

THE TREE WAS SO DISTRESSED
WITNESSING SUCH SORROW AND PAIN
GOD MADE THE DOGWOOD A PROMISE
NEVER AGAIN TO WITNESS SUCH SHAME.

HENCEFORTH, SMALL AND SLENDER
PETALS, TWO LONG AND TWO SHORT
USING CENTER THORNS FOR A CROWN
A STORY TO STIR YOUR HEART.

A SYMBOL OF THE CROSS
IT'S BEAUTY, UN-DENIED
FOR FORGIVENESS OF SINS
JESUS BLED, AND DIED

OUR LIFE IS LIKE A VAPOR
BLOSSOMS BLOOM, AND QUICKLY DIE
WE CAN KNOW PEACE AND COMFORT
FROM OUR HEAVENLY FATHER, ON HIGH.

[10] In back of Pat and Don's house there is a beautiful Dogwood Tree. Each spring it provides beautiful white blossoms.

Pat And Bear Going Fishing

"Miss Pat thinks we are going fishing. The joke is on her. Not today. I have other ideas. 'Cause I'm hungry as a bear."

Pat and Sammy in Avalanche/pick-up

Printed in the United States
By Bookmasters